WOMEN'S HISTORY RESOURCES

at the

State Historical Society of Wisconsin

WOMEN'S HISTORY RESOURCES

at the

State Historical Society of Wisconsin

by

James P. Danky
Christine M. Rongone
Beverly L. Youtz
Eleanor McKay
Christine I. Schelshorn
Maxine Fleckner

Fourth Edition

Revised and Enlarged

State Historical Society of Wisconsin
Madison : 1982

Copyright 1982 by
The State Historical Society of Wisconsin
All rights reserved
Cover design by Judy Patenaude

Library of Congress Cataloging in Publication Data:

Wisconsin. State Historical Society. Women's history.

Includes index.

1. Women--United States--History--Sources.
2. Bibliography--Bibliography--Women--North America.
3. Library resources on Women--North America.
4. Women--North America--Bibliography--Catalogs.
5. Wisconsin. State Historical Society. I. Danky, James Philip, 1947- II. Title.
Z7961.A1W57 1981 [HQ1426] 016.30141'2 79-17522
ISBN 0-87020-189-1

Alternative Cataloging in Publication Data:

Women's history: resources at the State Historical Society of Wisconsin. By James P. Danky and others. 4th ed., reviewed and enlarged. Madison, State Historical Society of Wisconsin, 1982.
1. Women--United States--History--Archival resources.
2. Women--United States--History--Library resources.
3. Wisconsin. State Historical Society. 4. Women--United States--History--Sources. I. Wisconsin. State Historical Society. II. Danky, James P., 1947- compiler.
016.3014129 or 301.4129'016

For

Beverly L. Youtz

1947 - 1979

BASIC INFORMATION

Located on the University of Wisconsin-Madison campus at 816 State Street (at the corner of Park and Langdon streets, eight blocks west of the State Capitol), the State Historical Society of Wisconsin is open to the public without charge. Automobile parking in the campus area is a problem. All-day or five-hour facilities are usually filled by mid-morning. The Memorial Union lot on Langdon Street, the Helen C. White Hall garage on Park Street (across from the Union), and the Lake Street Ramp have all-day parking. Street parking, when available, is limited by two-hour meters. A researcher may obtain a one-day or one-week visitor's parking permit from the University Parking Office (263-6666). A campus bus (30¢) runs about every ten minutes between outlying parking lots and the campus, and city buses (55¢) run between the campus area and all sections of Madison. Within a few minutes' walk from the Society are the Madison Inn and Town/Campus Motel and a variety of meal facilities ranging from snack bars to restaurants. Within about a mile other hotels and motels may be reached by longer walks or by bus. Detailed suggestions for housing are available upon request from the Reference Archivist. If you are planning a visit from some distance we strongly urge you to write or telephone ahead in order to avoid disappointment.
Hours: The Library is normally open 8 a.m. to 9 p.m., Monday through Thursday, and 8 a.m. to 5 p.m., Friday and Saturday. The Archives Division Reading Room, including the Map Section, is normally open from

8 a.m. to 5 p.m., Monday through Saturday. The Iconographic Collections Study Room is open 8 a.m. to 5 p.m., Monday through Friday. Exceptions occur most frequently on Saturdays during the summer and during the University's recess periods. Detailed schedules are posted or will be mailed on request. The Film Archive is open Monday through Friday from 8:30 a.m. to 4:30 p.m. Only Museum exhibits are open on Sunday.

Telephone Numbers:

Archives

Reference	(608) 262-3338
Iconographic Collections	(608) 262-9581
Maps	(608) 262-5867

Library

Circulation	(608) 262-3421
Reference	(608) 262-9590
Newspapers/Periodicals	(608) 262-9584
Government Publications	(608) 262-2781

Museum

(608) 262-2704

Film Archives

(608) 262-0585

Mailing Address:

    816 State Street
    Madison, Wisconsin 53706

TABLE OF CONTENTS

Basic Information	v
Introduction	1
The Library	4
The Archives	15
Labor Collections	21
Social Action	26
Theater Collections	29
Mass Communications	32
Wisconsin Manuscripts	34
Draper and McCormick Manuscripts	39
Public Records	42
Iconographic Collections	47
The Museum	63
Film Archive, Wisconsin Center for Film and Theater Research	66
Afterword	72
Appendix	74
About Contributors	77

Illustrations follow page 54

INTRODUCTION

The recent interest in women's history has presented problems for historians which parallel those faced by many minority, urban, and working-class historical researchers: the lack of access to documentation. A further problem for many researchers is readily available access, particularly to archival resources. This shortcoming has resulted from many collecting agencies using traditional formats and gathering traditional types of items. The outcome has been a lack of materials appropriate to the research task. The State Historical Society of Wisconsin constitutes one exception to this general pattern. Since its founding 135 years ago, the Society has fortuitously collected printed materials, manuscripts, archival materials, pictures, and museum artifacts which detail the accomplishments and status of women in North American society. However, materials are often segregated by format and consequently are spread throughout many of the Society's Divisions. Researchers must consider using the resources of several divisions to cover many topics adequately.

The Society's third salaried employee (after Lyman Copeland Draper and Daniel Steele Durrie) was Isabel Durrie, the daughter of Daniel, who was hired as assistant librarian in 1870. Since that time the Society has been fortunate to have had on its staff uncounted women who helped it achieve prominence through their managerial and scholarly talents.

Annie B. Nunns, whose fifty-four-year career at the Society began in 1889 under Reuben Gold Thwaites and

1

ended during World War II, was assistant superintendent for more than half that time and was responsible for the Society's operations. Women's commitment to historical agencies and preservation is evidenced by the activities of others, including Iva Welsh, Mary Foster, Minnie Oakley, Emma Hawley, Lillian Beecroft, Anna Evans, Ruth Davis, Livia Appel, Lillian Krueger, Monica Staedtler, Dorothy Park, Lucille Kellar, Mary Tuohy Ryan, Margaret Gleason, Florence Baker, Georgiana Sheldon, Emma Gattiker, Jean Cady, Esther DeBoos, Ruth Hayward, Ruth Shuttleworth, Sophie Brewer, Litta Bascom, Verena Barlow, Daisy Beecroft, Martha Edwards, Doris Platt, and Mabel Marks, all of whom worked in varying administrative, professional, and scholarly capacities for many years.

Scholarly publishing by women at the Society is a more publicized and perhaps better-known indication of their importance. Emma Blair's work with Thwaites on the Jesuit Relation (1898-1900), Newspaper Catalog (1898), and her translation of Nicholas Perrot's narrative are monuments to scholarship. Ada Tyng Griswold's 1911 catalog of the newspaper collection is still considered one of the best ever executed. Louise Phelps Kellogg, a student of Frederick Jackson Turner's and the first woman president of the Mississippi Valley Historical Association (later the Organization of American Historians), was senior research associate for many years and published widely, her best-known works being The French Regime in Wisconsin and the Northwest (1925) and The British Regime in Wisconsin and the Northwest (1935). (Dr. Kellogg's career was analyzed in David Kinnett's "Miss Kellogg's Quiet Passion," published in the Summer, 1979, issue of the Wisconsin Magazine of History.) Guides to the Society's manuscript collections have been compiled by Alice E. Smith and Josephine L. Harper, while guides to individual collections (such as the McCormick Collection guide by Margaret Hafstad) have been executed by other women. Alice E. Smith's The History of Wisconsin, Volume 1: From Exploration to Statehood

(1973) was the first of a six-volume set on the state and has received exceptionally favorable scholarly notices and a remarkable public reception. Much of it was serialized in the Milwaukee Journal concurrent with publication. Smith, the long-time head of research at the Society, produced many other volumes of distinction including James Duane Doty: Frontier Promoter (1954) and George Smith's Money: a Scottish Investor in America (1966). A full bibliography of Smith's works appears in the Wisconsin Magazine of History (49:162-63, Winter, 1965-66).

THE LIBRARY

The Society's Library contains excellent primary and secondary women's history sources. The collection has been developed, generally, without a sexual bias, but with the frequent result that pertinent materials have not been segregated into a particular physical area or unit. The Library has a divided catalog, unlike the integrated ones found in many libraries, and basic access to the Library's collection is through it. The public catalog contains the following files: author-title, subject, newspaper, directory, broadside chronology, Wisconsin place names, and index to Wisconsin in newspapers and periodicals to 1955. The author-title and subject catalogs contain entries for the Society's collection of over one and a half million books, pamphlets, clippings, microforms, and periodicals, including many government publications. For pre-1967 acquisitions, separate title entries were not always made, so knowing an author's name speeds the task of locating items.

A separate catalog in the Microforms Reading Room must be used to determine the status of a particular reel (positive or negative microfilm) and to learn reel or item numbers, although the Microforms Catalog duplicates the bibliographic information in the public catalog. A program has been begun to integrate newspaper titles into the author-title catalog, whereas before they were available only in the newspaper catalog. But until this project is completed, the best guide to newspaper holdings is the newspaper catalog, which is arranged alphabetically by state and city,

then alphabetically by title within each city. The
Library's broadside collection is fully cataloged in
the author-title and subject catalogs, but a separate
chronological file is maintained as a part of the public catalog. Additional broadsides of primarily pictorial importance may be found in the Iconography Collections, discussed later.

The Map Section's catalog, located in the Archives
Division Reading Room, contains atlas, plat book, and
sheet map entries. The separate directory catalog
lists nearly 6,000 directories and is arranged geographically by state and city, then chronologically
within cities. The Wisconsin Place Names Catalog was
compiled by staff members many years ago and is
arranged alphabetically by the name of the area.
Occasionally new entries are added by the reference
librarian. Information on the origin of hundreds of
names (some were named after or by women, e.g. Almena
and Arcadia) and place locations were gleaned from
local histories. More up-to-date and comprehensive
locational information is provided in the Atlas of
Wisconsin (1974). The index to "Wisconsin in Newspapers and Periodicals to 1955" was an on-going project of the Library staff until budgetary considerations forced termination. The arrangement is by subject (Women in Wisconsin, Societies) with references
to specific newspaper or periodical articles.

The Library's subject catalog uses the Library of
Congress system of subject headings. The heading of
first importance to check is "women." Under this subject the subdivisions of particular note to the historian are: "social conditions," "history" (which is
further divided chronologically), "societies and
clubs," and "health and hygiene." Religious groups
are indicated using a comma instead of a hyphen, as in
"women, Jewish" or "women, Hindu." Some headings lead
researchers directly to the more specialized field,
such as "women and socialism," "Afro-American women,"
or "women teachers." The evolution of subject headings can adversely affect the researcher who fails to

5

pay the strictest attention. One example is the shift from "women--teachers" to "women teachers" in recent years. Because the subject "women" is not always indicated in the cataloging, other subjects must be searched if one is to locate appropriate materials. These would include headings for organizations in which women played an important role, such as the Amalgamated Clothing Workers, the Packinghouse Workers, the Mormon church, and various benevolent and philanthropic groups. Additionally, consulting the subdivision "biography" under general headings such as religious groups will reveal materials on women where the subdivision for women has not been used. The serious researcher should consult each catalog and should be systematic, imaginative, and thorough. If this advice results in conflicting information or confusion, patrons should consult a library staff member.

While the Society's collections are strong for most topics, some are particularly so. These include: frontier/utopian communities, ethnic groups, women's organizations, women and labor unions in the 1930's to 1950's, women's political groups outside the mainstream, professional organizations, mass communications and performing arts, county and local politics and education, non-Lutheran Protestant churches, charitable groups, reform movements, family life, spiritualism, genealogy, and anthropology.

For information about the holdings of other libraries, whose collections are more comprehensive than the Society's in some area, the researcher has access to other libraries' printed guides and catalogs housed at the Society. Three pamphlets report on the Sophia Smith Collections at Smith College in Northampton, Massachusetts, while three large volumes of printed catalogs of Radcliffe College's Arthur and Elizabeth Schlesinger Library on the History of Women in America describe its books, manuscripts, and pictures.

Beyond the descriptive materials about the holdings of other institutions, the Society's Library has obtained microfilm copies of manuscript materials held in many repositories around the United States. These include, for example, the scrapbooks of Susan B. Anthony (7 reels), the complete trial materials of California vs. Angela Davis (12 reels), and the organizational records of the National Woman's Party Papers (276 reels). The papers of prominent women held in microform include those of Mary McLeod Bethune (1 reel), Carrie Chapman Catt (18 reels), Lydia Maria Child (97 microfiche), Isabella Beecher Hooker (145 microfiche), Elizabeth Cady Stanton (5 reels), and Frances Marion Streamer (1 reel). The Raya Dunayevskaya Collection (2 reels) provides another source for the study of communism when compared to the Society's collection of the papers of Betty Gannett, which is also available on microfilm (17 reels). Oral history transcripts, in both bound volumes and microformats, are available from many other repositories including the Schlesinger Library and the University of California's Bancroft Library.

Since the time of Lyman Draper, newspapers have formed an important part of the collection, and the Society now has one of the five largest collections of newspapers in the United States. Wisconsin newspapers, colonial and early American newspapers, territorial newspapers, Civil War newspapers, and labor newspapers have been emphasized. In addition, the Library maintains a collection of dailies from several metropolitan areas. Since 1954 the University of Wisconsin and the Society libraries have divided collecting functions. This division means that certain categories of women's publications are in the Memorial Library (gay or lesbian publications) and in the College of Agriculture's Steenbock Library (<u>Ladies' Home Journal</u> and similar publications). The Society has some earlier mass-circulation magazines for women such as <u>Godey's Magazine</u>.

Early in the nineteenth century women began to obtain jobs on newspapers, usually as typesetters and infrequently as reporters and editors. By the Civil War era some females, like Sophia Bloomer of the

Richland Zouave, edited Wisconsin newspapers, primarily in smaller communities. Harriet Baker Cramer began as a typesetter on the Evening Wisconsin in Milwaukee and later married the publisher. After his death in 1905 she continued to publish this important paper. A careful inspection of the index in Donald Oehlerts' Guide to Wisconsin Newspapers (1958) reveals names of other women editors and publishers, including Ella Beierle (Mercer News), Carla Spalthoff (La Farge Enterprise), and Mabel Hansen (Hartland News). Further, women often assisted their editor-publisher husbands without receiving masthead credit. The Proceedings of the Wisconsin Editorial Association contain annual lists of participants, including women, and may be searched profitably.

The Society has always collected the publications of movement organizations beginning with women's suffrage activities in the mid-nineteenth century. Some of the more interesting titles include: The Wisconsin Citizen, The Revolution, and New Era. Today's women's publications differ from their predecessors in several respects: they are less frequently oriented to a single issue, and they are usually edited by women. (Many suffragist periodicals were edited by men.) The development of modern women's papers, which often focus on inequities in modern American society, was encouraged by movements like the various civil rights efforts with their goal of equality. Representative newspapers include Off Our Backs and Women in Action. The Library's collection of contemporary women's papers has been enlarged by the 850 titles in the Herstory microfilm collections, based on the closed Women's History Library of Berkeley, California. The Society's collection and those of other area libraries are described in Women's Periodicals and Newspapers from the 18th Century to 1981: A Union List of the Holdings of Madison, Wisconsin Libraries (1982) edited by James P. Danky and compiled by Maureen E. Hady, Barry Christopher Noonan, and Neil E. Strache.

The publications of government agencies are often

overlooked by historians, but they constitute invaluable resources for women's history. The Society collects documents issued by the United States government, the Canadian government, the fifty states and territories, the Canadian provinces, Wisconsin counties, and selected Wisconsin municipalities. The Society is a depository for United States federal and Wisconsin state publications. Some government items not available at the Society but relating to women may be found at appropriate University of Wisconsin-Madison campus libraries, such as The Center for Health Sciences Library and the Steenbock Agricultural Library.

The basic tool for locating the publications of the United States government is the Monthly Catalog of United States Government Publications. Each issue is indexed and the December issue contains an index for each calendar year. Related indexes like the Decennial Cumulative Indexes, Cumulative Subject Index 1900-1971, the Decennial Cumulative Personal Author Indexes 1941-1970, and the Cumulative Title Index 1789-1976 (the first volume of which has just been published) will assist the researcher. All but the last two should be treated as subject indexes because there are few entries under the names of issuing agencies. Congressional reports and documents can be located by subject through the twelve-part CIS U.S. Serial Set Index.

The federal government, the largest gatherer of data in the U.S., has long collected statistics which happened to include women as a category. The Department of Labor's Women's Bureau, established in 1920, has collected increasingly extensive statistics on women. The current women's movement has sparked the collection, analysis, and publication of works treating women as a special topic to a greater extent than ever before.

Other federal agencies dealing with women include the Department of Health, Education, and Welfare, the Bureau of the Census, and the Civil Rights Commission, as well as the various commissions on women. These include the President's Commission on the Status of Women, the Citizen's Advisory Council on the Status of Women, the National Commission on the Observance of International Women's Year in 1975, and the National Advisory Council on Women's Educational Programs. In the legislative branch, appropriate bills such as the Nineteenth Amendment (giving women the right to vote) can be researched through the hearings, committee reports, and Congressional Record published by Congress. Reaction by state governments to national issues such as the Equal Rights Amendment (the proposed Twenty-Seventh Amendment) can be observed by studying the journals and reports of the fifty states. By 1967 most states had commissions on the status of women prompted by the President's Commission on the Status of Women.

Wisconsin state publications concerning women are fewer in number than those of the federal government, but they do provide local details not found elsewhere. The publications of the Governor's Commission on the Status of Women, and those of the Department of Industry, Labor and Human Relations, the Department of Health and Social Services, and the Governor's Commission on Human Rights contain a great deal of material about women. There is even an early twentieth-century report on Wisconsin's "white slave trade" (the so-called Teasdale Commission's report).

The bibliographic apparatus for state and local government publications is developed to a much lesser extent than that for federal government publications. There is no comprehensive subject index. Most states published their early material in collected documents series, which bound all state agencies' publications together by year rather than separating into volumes by agency. One analytical index to these publications which includes information on women is the Index of Economic Materials in State Documents . This index, arranged by general topic, covers thirteen states through 1904. Material on women is included mostly under topics other than women; for example an article "On poor pay of female teachers in Kentucky" contained in the annual report of the superintendent of common schools bound in the 1843 collected documents of Kentucky is listed under "Labor--Wages--Teachers" in this index.

Indexes prepared by states for their own publications vary in comprehensiveness and beginning publication dates. General access to publications from other states is available through the shelflist, which may be consulted with the assistance of the government publications reference librarian. The shelflist is arranged by key word of the publishing agency, which is in effect a limited subject approach. The shelflist also contains analytics of major series in the collected documents as well as cards for later publications issued separately. The major point of access for Wisconsin local government publications is also the shelflist.

Access to Canadian federal government publications is available through the Canadian Government Publications Catalogue. Canadian provincial publications are best approached through the shelflist.

Because of the multiple but non-comprehensive points of access to government publications, reference assistance should be sought from the government publications reference librarian.

Like most historical agencies, the Society documents influential, prominent, or wealthy women and their activities better than it furnishes evidence about ordinary women. But by analyzing such resources as city directories and the census, historians could produce and have produced meaningful urban and working-class histories. (Women's ownership of property could be examined through archival resources as well, especially through tax and probate records, for example.)

Census records of the State and Territory of Wisconsin and of the federal government are available in part through the library with originals of the state

censuses housed in the Archives Division.
In territorial Wisconsin a census was taken whenever there was an attempt to change the status of the area: 1836, 1838, 1842, 1846, 1847. From 1836 to 1847 the census listed only the heads of households, who would only occasionally be female, and then they can be sometimes disguised through the use of initials instead of given names. The 1850 United States census, the first to list by name all those living within state boundaries, is valuable for its information about gender, age, national origin, and the status and occupations of men but not women. Occupations of many adults are listed; and servants and boarders are listed after the head of the household, women members of the family, and children. About 300,000 people lived in Wisconsin at the time of the census of 1850, and that census can be used to infer the status of women. From 1855-1895 the state took a census, by head of household only, every decade on the fifth year; in 1905 it took a complete name census. From 1850 to the present the federal government has taken a census every decade on the tenth year. The Wisconsin censuses for 1820 through 1870 are indexed by individual name and are microfilmed as are the indexes; these indexes, however, must be used with care and often with creativity, because the spelling of even English names is frequently erratic. The 1880 census is not indexed in the same manner, but rather a "soundex" index (a special aural index) on microfilm assists in locating individuals by surname. A guide to using the "soundex" index appears at the beginning of each reel and is available in the Microforms Reading Room. The 1905 census, which is also on microfilm, was the first state census to provide extensive information on all residents. Since 1977 the Library has been engaged in creating a personal name index to the 1905 Census and expects to complete this project in late 1982. To date, all of the names have been transcribed and county-by-county alphabetic indexes are available on microfilm for fifty-nine of Wiscon-

sin's seventy-one counties.

Either in manuscript, print, or on microfilm, the Historical Society has at least one form of the federal population schedules for Wisconsin for 1820-1900. The 1890 schedules for Wisconsin and most other states were destroyed accidentally by fire in Washington. Census records to 1880 for all the states are available at the Society. The Society holds the 1900 census only for Wisconsin. In addition printed statistical compendia for censuses through 1970 are found in the Government Publications Section, and those for the 1980 census are being added as they appear.

Twenty years ago women's history consisted of biographical sketches of "notable women" and studies of selected social movements with which women had been traditionally associated. Historians detailed the activities of a Jane Addams or an Eleanor Roosevelt, described the exploits of a Molly Pitcher or a Sacajawea, and recounted women's involvement in the abolition, temperance, and suffrage movements. But with these few exceptions, women's contributions and participation in American life were either under-represented or ignored.

Events of the 1960's helped change this and encouraged the development of a new women's history, a history in which women's roles in society and their effects on the political, social, and economic structure were recognized and studied. The rapidly changing and often turbulent political and social climate of the decade helped to bring about this more sophisticated appreciation of women's history. A resurgent civil rights movement shattered the image of homogeneous American people and encouraged racial and ethnic groups to emphasize those traits which made them distinctive. Women, as a group, developed a similar sense of identity. Demands for changes in the existing political and social structure often went hand-in-hand with a growing opposition to the war in Vietnam, which demonstrated the effectiveness of grassroots organizations. Within a socially active milieu a more vigorous women's movement emerged. Betty Friedan published The Feminine Mystique in 1963, giving the movement a portion of its philosophical basis as it encouraged people to question traditional roles and to seek new alternatives. It also promoted extensive media coverage with vastly differing degrees of interpretation. Sara Evans in Personal Politics: The Roots of Women's Liberation in the Civil Rights Movement and the New Left (1979), among other later authors, outlined the rise of the new women's movement, "women's liberation," in the context of the civil rights and new left activities. Historians, in turn, responded to all of these developments and began to re-examine women's role in history. Expanding historical methodologies and sophisticated quantitative research techniques borrowed from other disciplines aided historians, who were now able to study the movement and actions of average men and women rather than focus exclusively on elite groups. Not only were conventional topics subject to new analyses, but women's interaction with the social, economic, and political world also were seen in new light. Gradually women were acknowledged as an integral part of America's past.

THE ARCHIVES

To assist researchers in this study of women, the Archives Division has extensive holdings of private and public records. It is a major repository for manuscript collections of private individuals and organizations and for records of Wisconsin state, county, and local governmental agencies. These holdings afford researchers a variety of approaches in their study of women. Source materials may include correspondence, minutes, diaries, financial records, legal documents, reports, clippings, speeches, writings, genealogical materials, scrapbooks, news releases, reminiscences, notes, and other record forms, depending upon the type of collection consulted.

Relevant private records include both those created by women and those relating to them. Obvious sources are those collections created by individual women or their organizations. In addition, materials generated by women are often located in other types of collections. For example, papers from female relatives, friends, or acquaintances may constitute a section of a "man's" collection. Family papers usually will contain documents from a wife, sister, mother, or daughter, while organizational records may include materials from a woman executive, administrator, or secretary. Unfortunately, these types of sources for women's materials are often overlooked by finding aids and researchers alike. In addition to papers by women, the manuscripts or private papers relating to women or concerning their lives are nearly endless. Correspondence written by men may reveal their opinions on a wide spectrum of topics such as suffrage, abortion, affirmative action, no-fault divorce, the family, the working wife, child-rearing practices, or the women's movement in general and offer an opportunity to compare and contrast men's and women's perceptions of these issues. Records of organizations which directly affect women, such as hospitals or schools, also deserve inspection. Sample topics might include a historical study of the types of health care or education women received through time, a comparative analysis of the treatment of men and women by these institutions, or the roles and attitudes these two professions played as major employers of women.

Likewise, public records provide a rich, though often forgotten, source for the study of women. Women have directly participated in government both as salaried employees and as elected officials, and frequently their records are preserved. Their involvement as concerned constituents seeking to affect policy may be found in agency files. The human services and regulatory functions that are of particular concern to women, such as welfare, widow's pensions, and the regulation or licensing of nurses, day care centers, and hairdressers, are also part of the public record. In fact, access to "women's collections" in both private and public holdings is limited only by the defined research topic and the imagination and persistence of the researcher.

The Society has collected private records since its founding. Its first secretary, Lyman Copeland Draper, actively solicited manuscript collections with which to document Wisconsin's early history and sought to preserve a written record of the state's economic, political, social, and cultural activities. Draper's personal research collection--the Draper Collection--was transferred to the Society in the 1890's; it documents various aspects of the trans-Allegheny frontier from 1750-1815. It remains one of the Society's most heavily used collections. Also notable is the

McCormick Collection, consisting of a series of papers of individuals, companies, and organizations associated with Cyrus H. McCormick, the inventor of the reaper. In recent years contemporary collecting areas have been developed to complement the general Wisconsin, Draper, and McCormick collections. Thus, in the areas of labor, social action, mass communications, and theater, the Society today seeks the records of prominent individuals and organizations at both the state and national level. This concentrated focus gives collecting areas an added strength, as the same people, events, and issues may be discussed in many different collections, permitting researchers to sample various individual viewpoints and to compare both local and national perspectives.

However, despite the richness of these holdings, manuscript collections typically do not provide a long perspective over time. Because they are dependent upon individual people or organizations for their creation and maintenance, they provide comparatively fragmented documentation. To offset this characteristic, public records can be used to complement and supplement these private records. Though often less individually detailed than manuscripts, public records may describe the broad fabric of society in ways that private records cannot. In theory they provide a greater continuity, as governmental functions—despite personnel changes or departmental reorganizations—tend to be constant. In fact, however, many agency records found in the state archives are fragmentary, particularly those of the nineteenth and early twentieth centuries. It was not until 1947 that the Society became the official depository of state records, and, prior to that time, many public records were destroyed by natural causes or by the neglect or ignorance of their keepers. Today, through the cooperative efforts of local, county, and state officials, documents of permanent value are transferred to the Archives, thus creating another major source of documentation of which researchers need to be aware.

A problem arises in trying to identify "women's collections" even if a definition of the subject is agreed upon. Part of the problem is inherent in the nature of archival materials. Records are retained as organic units, and the researchers must be sufficiently sophisticated to use existing finding aids and to couple them with an imaginative knowledge of their subject areas so they can locate the specific information sought. With women's history, as with any changing field of study, the problem of access is more difficult, for finding aids never fully reflect new topics or anticipate future research needs. It is only in recent years that an attempt has been made to provide access to women's collections as an identifiable group. The manuscript catalog now lists entries for subjects such as "woman," "woman--history and conditions of women," "woman--professions and employment," and "woman--rights of women." However, catalog access to the majority of private papers by and about women remains by collection title and by general Library of Congress subject headings. Among relevant subject terms under which researchers may find "women's" papers are "abortion," "aged," "ballet," "beauty shops," "birth control," "day nurseries," "divorce," "family," "hairdressing," "human relations," "interior decorators," "librarians and libraries," "nurses and nursing," "pornography," and "witchcraft." As a supplement to the standard finding aids, researchers also should consult with the reference archivists whose cumulative knowledge of our public and private holdings may be able to save considerable time in locating appropriate records. Processing archivists, who initially organize and describe the papers, may also be able to provide assistance.

The finding aids for private records include the Society's guides, registers, and card catalog. A three-volume general guide, <u>Guide to the Manuscripts of the State Historical Society of Wisconsin</u>, describes the manuscript holdings to 1965. Additional guides have been issued for some of the specialized collecting areas such as A Guide to Labor Papers in the State Historical Society of Wisconsin and Sources for Mass Communications, Film and Theater Research: A Guide. Other subject guides which contain descriptions of women's records are the Guide to the Wisconsin Jewish Archives, the Guide to Historical Resources in Milwaukee Area Archives, and the numerous guides describing the holdings of the Area Research Centers, listed on page 101. Published guides to selected microfilm editions of papers also have been issued. Among these publications are The Records of the Committee to Secure Justice for Morton Sobell, The Papers of Betty Gannett, The Papers of Robert Marion La Follette, Sr., The Papers of the University Settlement Society of New York City, and the forthcoming guide to the Draper Collection. Though relatively few collections possess published guides, most manuscript collections are accompanied by a descriptive register detailing the individual's biography or the organization's history and the scope and content of the papers. A dictionary card catalog provides subject, title, and donor access to these registers.

To researchers accustomed to finding aids in a catalog format, access to state records may initially appear confusing. But, as with manuscripts, access to women's materials is dependent upon a series of finding aids and the knowledge of the reference and processing archivists. Finding aids may include guides, Kardex descriptions, and inventories. The Guide to the Wisconsin State Archives provides a comprehensive description of the state's permanently valuable records. Although published in 1966 and no longer current, its index provides the only subject access available to the state archives. A new edition is planned for 1983. Kardex cards provide brief descriptions of record series and detail their contents and general arrangement. (A record series is an organic unit comparable to a manuscripts collection.) Should an occasional series warrant a more detailed description, an inventory is produced. County and local records are described similarly in a descriptive card catalog format, again with an inventory used as an occasional supplement. There is, at this time, no subject access to these latter holdings.

Some of these records, both public and private, are kept at one of the Area Research Centers (ARC's). Located on the four-year campuses of the University of Wisconsin and at Northland College, the thirteen centers consitute a statewide network of regional repositories which house collections having a regional or local focus. In a further attempt to make these records more readily accessible, most are also available for loan for use either in the Archives Division in Madison or in the research rooms at the various centers. In addition, many of the ARC's, including Eau Claire, Green Bay, La Crosse, Milwaukee, Oshkosh, Parkside, Platteville, River Falls, Stevens Point, and Stout, have produced separate guides or checklists to their archival and manuscript holdings. (For complete bibliographic information, see Appendix.) An examination of these more recent finding aids may reveal additional women's materials not found in other, older sources.

The remainder of this section describes the variety of source material available in both private and public records. Among the private papers discussed will be four major collecting areas--labor, social action, mass communications, and theater--and the general Wisconsin, Draper, and McCormick collections. In public records the focus will be on the state archives and county and local records. The aim is not to provide a definitive listing of every relevant collection in each category, but rather to mention broad groupings of appropriate records, to give examples of them, and to suggest possible areas of research. More detailed descriptions are available in the previously described guides. In addition, several of the cited collections are described in Women's History Sources: A Guide to Archives and Manuscript Collections in the

United States (R. R. Bowker, New York, 1979). Researchers wishing to obtain additional information regarding these collections should contact the reference archivist. A few of the records are restricted and may require special permission to use.

Labor Collections

Women have always worked and have participated in the labor movement since its earliest days. Brought into the work force during the initial stages of industrialization as a source of cheap labor, women became the backbone of factories and mills where they, along with others, were routinely exploited. Concentrated in low-paying jobs, excluded from many other types of work, offered little or no job mobility, and often subjected to poor working conditions, women were sympathetic to the appeals of the labor movement.

With the passage of years women enjoyed some degree of advancement. In fact they came to dominate certain careers or professions such as nursing, teaching, and secretarial work. However, even in these fields women were often excluded from administrative positions or else received less pay than men doing identical work. Wartime afforded many women opportunities to expand into non-traditional areas as they were recruited by industry to replace men who had gone to war. These opportunities were usually short-lived, for when the men returned and resumed their careers women often lost their paying jobs and returned to their homes. Documentation of women's participation in the labor movement and the labor movement's response to the plight of women workers can be found in many of the Society's labor collections.

These labor holdings trace the development of the labor movement and trade unionism as a worker response to industrialization. Included in the collections are the papers of local unions, trade councils and other state labor organizations, and the personal papers of socialists, labor leaders, and labor economists. The direct participation of women in the movement may be studied in the papers (1917-1923)* of author and socialist Elizabeth Gurley Flynn, who, as an organizer for the Workers Defense Union, worked on behalf of individuals accused of political crimes, labor agitation, or subversion during the Red Scare of the 1920's. On a more theoretical level the papers (1896-1933) of Helen Sumner Woodbury document her career as a government labor economist who was also active in the Bureau of Industrial Research and the Brookings Institution. Another woman whose administrative efforts furthered the labor cause is Toni Sender. Her collection (1934-1964) of correspondence, reports, and speeches, describes her work as a delegate for the International Confederation of Free Trade Unions at the United Nations. Efforts by women to educate and organize themselves can be seen in the records of the American Labor Education Service (1921-1951) and the Milwaukee Chapter of the Women's Trade Union League (1948-1956). The former collection documents several early experiments in worker education and includes the records of the Bryn Mawr Summer School for Women Workers in Industry. Founded in 1921 by N. Carey Thomas, former president of Bryn Mawr College, the School attempted to develop educational programs specifically geared toward working women. Activities of labor-conscious women may also be seen in the records of the Milwaukee chapter of the Women's Trade Union League, which promoted equality of women and trade unionism. Records of national and local unions can document the entry of women into new occupational fields, their general performance on the job, and the success or failure of organized labor to respond to women's needs. Larger labor collections provide insight into general work conditions, wages,

*All dates cited refer to the dates spanned by the papers, not to the birth and death dates of individuals or organizations.

specific grievances, and the general collective bargaining process. For example, a study of maternity leave grievances and their resolution would be a contribution to women's studies. Records of unions in which women comprise the majority of the membership, such as the teaching profession or the textile industry, are particularly helpful in studying women's history. Among these represented in our collections are the American Federation of Hosiery Workers (1913, 1923-1964), the Textile Workers Union of America (1915-1976), Madison Teachers Incorporated (1960-1975), and the Wisconsin Education Association Council (1853-1975).

Women's interest in bettering society and improving the lives of individuals has led to their long-standing involvement in several diverse movements of social change. The Society's holdings in this area date from early movements such as suffrage, peace, and temperance, through more contemporary social actions such as the civil rights and anti-war movements. Many women simultaneously participated in several causes. These collections afford an opportunity to study individual activist women; their social, economic, and political backgrounds and belief systems which fostered their activism; and those unique characteristics which resulted in selective participation in these movements by some women.

The struggle for women's rights and for political equality was of concern to some women since the country's founding. But it was not until 1920 that women --at least white women--were granted their voting rights with the passage of the Nineteenth Amendment. Of potential interest to researchers are materials on women who actively sought this right, the political and organizational skills they exhibited, and the related women's rights issues that often accompanied the suffragists' primary concern. The papers (1816-1952) of reformer, humanitarian, and pacifist Ada James document her tenure as president of the Political Equality League, a Wisconsin women's suffrage group;

her activity in the Woman's Party; and her involvement in movements advocating prohibition and birth control. Also included in the James Papers are proceedings (1885-1903) of the Wisconsin Woman Suffrage Association. The papers (1880-1968) of Gwyneth King Roe, a teacher of the Delsarte system of physical education, include correspondence, diaries, notes, and drafts of writings on suffrage, the Women's Peace Party, and freedom of dress for women. The papers (1861-1957) of Clara Bewick Colby, founder and editor of The Woman's Tribune, the recognized organization of the National Women Suffrage Association, include correspondence, a diary, lecture notes, writings, and materials from the Federal Suffrage Association, an organization in which Colby served as an officer. Among her correspondents are members of the National American Woman Suffrage Association, the International Woman Suffrage Alliance, and the Women's Freedom League. Interested in religion and philosophy, Colby wrote and spoke on the spiritual basis of the women's movement. Organizational records include those of the Wisconsin Woman's Suffrage Association (1897, 1904-1925), later reorganized as the League of Women Voters; these reveal the relationship of suffragists to political parties and other women's groups, their interest in progressive legislation, and their service during World War I.

  Although historically women have played a major, supportive role during wartime, by World War I some women began to organize the first peace societies. Their motivations varied. Some were inspired by humanistic concerns; others were driven by a simple desire to end the slaughter of brothers, sons, and husbands. Some saw the massive devastating nature of twentieth-century warfare as "masculinity run amuck." Among the relevant manuscript collections represented in the holdings are Julia Grace Wales' papers (1914-1917), which detail a plan for continuous mediation without an armistice, an idea which she developed in 1914; correspondence from several peace movement leaders from around the world are also contained in the collection. Zona Gale's papers (1838-1945) include both her literary works and her writings on behalf of women's suffrage, pacifism, world peace, prohibition, civil liberties, and racial equality. Papers (1881-1935) of Jessie Jack Hooper, Democratic party leader, candidate for the U.S. Senate in 1922, and first president of the Wisconsin League of Women Voters, reveal her involvement in both the suffrage and peace movements. Her letters with national and state officials concern the League of Nations, the World Court, the Kellogg-Briand Pact, the Pan-American Treaties, and proposals for a neutrality bill. Records (1924-1965) of the Madison chapter of the Women's International League for Peace and Freedom, which had its origin in a 1915 international women's congress to protest World War I, provide insight into women's lobbying efforts on behalf of disarmament measures, treaties, and cuts in military expenditures.

Another movement in which women played a driving force was temperance in use of alcohol. For many families, alcohol abuse went beyond the confines of personal tragedy to become an economic nightmare. The existing legal and economic structure prevented most women from controlling the breadwinning job or the resulting income. Perhaps the best-known organizational manifestation of the temperance movement was the Woman's Christian Temperance Union, which had chapters throughout the country. The Society has the records of several Wisconsin chapters which might lend themselves to a study of the variations in the goals and techniques employed by each chapter. In addition several small collections relating to women, such as Frances Willard (1858-1894) and Emilie C. Quiner (1861-1863), who were involved in the temperance movement, describe their activities and attitudes about the cause.

Social Action

Contemporary collections also reflect the social activism of women, particularly in the civil rights and anti-war movements of the 1960's. In addition to descriptions of dramatic human events involving such racially explosive issues as voter registration, desegregation of schools and housing, and equal job opportunities, the papers reflect the attitudes and motives of the people involved. A comparative study of the various civil rights organizations, showing their methods of decision making and the leadership roles (or lack thereof) assigned to women, could be accomplished by using several of these collections. For example, the papers (1964-1967) of New York City resident Jacqueline Bernard document her efforts to raise money and generate support for civil rights activities in Clay County, Mississippi. Miriam Feingold's papers (1960-1967) concern her activities as a member of the Southmore Political Action Club and as a worker for the Congress of Racial Equality (CORE) in Louisiana and Mississippi. Her journals and letters describe events such as freedom rides, demonstrations, and arrests, and detail their impact on civil rights workers participating in Mississippi summer projects which were designed to improve the status of the state's blacks. Another collection, the papers (1960-1966) of Jo Ann Ooiman Robinson, reveals her participation in the Mississippi Summer Project of 1964 which established freedom schools. The fall of the same year saw Robinson working on elections for the Agricultural Stabilization and Conservation Service and mobilizing support for the Freedom Democratic Party's challenge against regular delegates to the Democratic National Convention. Papers (1963-1967) of Elizabeth Sutherland relate exclusively to her book <u>Letters from Mississippi</u> (1965) which contains published letters from civil rights volunteers. Correspondence, notes, reports, and news releases (1963-1966) of civil rights activist

Lucille Montgomery show an early interest in the problems of literacy and poverty which ultimately led her into the civil rights movement, where she worked with the Student Non-Violent Coordinating Committee (SNCC). The Carl and Anne Braden Papers (1928-1972) extensively document their long careers as prominent activists in campaigns for civil rights and civil liberties. The Bradens worked as field organizers and later as executive directors for the Southern Conference Educational Fund (SCEF), a group that built white support for the civil rights movement. Organizational records include those of the Congress of Racial Equality (CORE), a civil rights group that sponsored a series of direct, non-violent actions such as sit-ins, freedom rides, and voter registration drives during the early 1960's. Their records consist of several distinct collections documenting the activities of its national office (1941-1967), regional offices (1948-1967), and largely autonomous local chapters (1953-1967). These records afford researchers an opportunity to do an in-depth study of CORE's tactics, including a detailed investigation of the role of women in this group.

The late 1960's were marked by campus unrest as student activists, using many of the same tactics earlier employed by the civil rights movement, protested both university and government policies. Much of their energies focused on the draft and the Vietnam War. Women comprised a large percentage of the college population and actively participated in these protests. The attitudes, influence, and leadership roles which women experienced in this movement are potential areas of study. A broader study, comparing the economic, social, and political backgrounds, motives, and goals of women civil rights and anti-war activists, might also prove interesting. The Todd Gitlin and Nanci Hollander collection (1961-1970) details the actions of an activist couple. Both were in the Students for a Democratic Society (SDS) of which Gitlin served as national president, the University of Michigan Friends of the Student Non-Violent Coordinating Committee

(SNCC), and other local and national activist groups. Records (1958-1970) from the national SDS office also provide a source for studying women's participation in a major radical organization which underwent a great amount of internal turmoil. Records (1968-1972) of the New University Conference concern a national organization of faculty, graduate students, and staff which encouraged radical research and scholarship. Of particular interest are the records of its Women's Caucus, formed to fight sex discrimination within both the organization itself and the university community in general. Examples of records of anti-war groups are the Citizens for Immediate Withdrawal of Madison, Wisconsin (1970-1971), Fifth Avenue Vietnam Peace Parade Committee (1965-1971), Madison Area Peace Action Council (1969-1973), Student Mobilization Committee to End the War in Vietnam (1966-1973), and others. All of these collections may contain some materials relating to their women members' activities. To augment the records of these anti-war groups, the Tere Rios Versace papers (1941-1977) offer another perspective on the war. The collection details the family's efforts to obtain information and the release of their son, Rocky, a prisoner of war who was later executed.

Women's increasing activism can also be seen in the rise of the feminist movement in which women began aggressively to seek an end to all types of discrimination based on sex and to lobby for programs geared to their special needs. Several small collections reflect women's interest in myriad topics such as rape, abortion, lesbianism, and the retention of their own surnames after marriage. Among these collections are the papers of Kathleen Nichol and Barbara Constans (1975-1979), Priscilla MacDougall (1972-1975), and the records of the Women's National Abortion Action Coalition (1969-1973). In addition, papers (1966-1972) of Joan Jordan, an author active in the women's movement in northern California, contain her correspondence with Pat Robinson, a prominent New York feminist, on abortion, birth control, child care centers, employment, racism, etc.

In addition to the major social movements discussed, women have expressed their interest in a variety of other reforms designed to improve the lot of humankind. Several women were involved in settlement work. Lizzie Black Kander's papers (1875-1960) discuss her social work among Russian Jewish immigrants who arrived in Milwaukee in the 1880's. She founded the Milwaukee Jewish Mission and helped finance the project by selling The Settlement Cookbook, initially composed of recipes from her cooking class, then going into many popular editions. Records (1886-1965) of the University Settlement Society of New York City provide an organizational perspective on the settlement phenomenon. Although most of the records were written by men, they do discuss subjects such as prostitution and women in the labor force. Another form of social work in which women were involved is the volunteer aid program movement here and abroad, including agencies like VISTA and the Peace Corps. Correspondence or diaries from Janet Davis (1964-1965), Donna Drewiske (1962-1964), Lea Heine (1966-1977), Laura Kiel (1963-1965), Janice Kneip (1962-1964), and Patricia Ann Silke (1962-1963) detail their activities and impressions of their work.

Other social action collections, too, show women's interest in civil liberties. Records (1946-1979) of the Committee to Secure Justice for Morton Sobell concern Helen Sobell's efforts to obtain a release from jail for her husband, who was imprisoned for espionage. They detail her successful efforts at mounting and sustaining a nationwide campaign aimed at his release, while their personal correspondence provides insight into imprisonment's effects on a marriage.

Theater Collections

Theater holdings, which focus on all phases of theater, motion picture, and television production in the

United States, comprise the third major collecting area. This is a joint program of the Society and the University of Wisconsin-Madison through the latter's Wisconsin Center for Film and Theater Research. The collections are many and varied, and reveal women's participation in all phases of behind-the-scenes production such as writing, directing, producing, lighting, and designing, as well as their work before the audience as actresses and performers. Scripts, found in many collections, provide a particularly rich source for the study of women, for the image of women which the media present not only reflects society's attitude toward women but also influences the responses and actions of its audience. Thus, media's impact is tremendous.

Personal papers containing scripts, correspondence, and scrapbooks of varying degrees of comprehensiveness exist for actresses Agnes Moorehead (1923-1974), Gale Sondergaard (1908-1964), June Havoc (1931-1963), and Kitty Carlisle (1922-1962). Costume designers are represented by Edith Head and Dorothy Jeakins. Papers (1934-1965) of Head, who won eight Academy Awards as one of the film industry's premier designers, include sketches and portions of her book The Dress Doctor (1959). The papers (1938-1973) of Dorothy Jeakins, who also designed primarily for motion pictures including Hawaii, The Music Man, and The Sound of Music, contain notes, workbooks, sketches, and photographs. Both collections are interesting not only for describing the careers of two successful women, but also as a source of information on changing women's fashions; for, unless a movie called for period costumes, women were usually costumed in the latest styles. Another important, though less well-known facet of show business can be found in the papers (1941-1966) of lighting designer Jean Rosenthal, who worked on theater and opera productions. Collections of women producers include those of Shirley Clarke (1949-1974) and Perry Miller Adato (1940-1974), both of whom have produced and directed documentaries. Also among the theater holdings are the collections of several women writers: Vera Caspary (1929-1968), author of Laura; Edna Ferber (1913-1963), Pulitzer Prize-winning author whose works include So Big, Show Boat, Cimmaron, and Giant; Katherine "Ketti" Frings (1921-1962), a novelist and playwright whose play Look Homeward Angel, based on Thomas Wolfe's novel, won a Pulitzer Prize for drama; Ruth Goodman Goetz (1916-1959), a playwright who often collaborated with her husband Augustus Goetz; Frances Goodrich (1927-1961), who in collaboration with her husband Albert Hackett earned a Pulitzer Prize for their stage adaptation of The Diary of Anne Frank and who wrote screenplays for The Thin Man series, Easter Parade, and Seven Brides for Seven Brothers; Jean Kerr (1929-1969), author and playwright whose works include her autobiographical book Please Don't Eat the Daisies and the play Mary, Mary; and Irna Phillips (1931-1968), a radio and television writer who originated the daytime soap opera format. This last collection is particularly interesting to students of women's history, for soap operas were specifically geared to an audience of housewives. Their scripts treated subjects which the writers and programmers believed would cater to women's particular interests and needs; and, in fact, soap operas explored myriad sensitive issues such as abortion, extra-marital affairs, and the plight of unwed mothers long before prime-time network television confronted these topics.

Organizational theatrical records in which materials on women can be found include those of MTM Enterprises, Inc. (1970-1978), United Artists (1919-1966), and the American Community Theatre Association (1965-1976). Although MTM's records do not document its corporate decision-making process, they do contain scripts, films, and prints from several television programs which the company produced, including The Bob Newhart Show, Rhoda, and The Mary Tyler Moore Show. The latter program focused on the life of an over-thirty, happily single working woman, Mary Richards. Earlier scripts present the more traditional charac-

terization of a woman--a passive individual who was
concerned about her marriage prospects. But, as the
show and character developed, Mary became more independent and concerns about her marital status faded.
The show, which enjoyed high ratings, provided writers
with a vehicle for presenting a new image of women and
viewers with an opportunity to see a successful woman
role model. Other MTM programs similarly portrayed
more liberated women characters. For United Artists,
a major film distribution company founded in 1919,
there is a massive collection of corporate records
which provide insight into the portrayal of women in
films themselves and in the advertising campaigns designed to promote the films. Moreover, one of United
Artists' founders and long-time officers was a woman,
Mary Pickford. Though better known as an actress,
Pickford was, in fact, an accomplished businesswoman,
and the records reveal her impact on United Artists'
corporate decisions and policies. Another collection
in which the activities of a woman administrator can
be seen is the American Community Theatre Association,
a national organization designed to serve groups and
individuals interested in community theater. Much of
the collection focuses on the period when Kay Fliehr
was either president or actively involved with the
group, and it reveals her abilities to organize and
stage national theatrical competitions.

Mass Communications

The final collecting area is the field of mass communications and consists of collections relating to
journalism, broadcasting, and advertising. Among the
women journalists whose papers record their work as
reporters are Dickey Chapelle (1933-1968), a freelance writer-photographer and one of the first journalists killed in Vietnam; Anne McCormick (1936-1954),
a foreign correspondent for The New York Times; Helen
Zotos (1947-1967), a news correspondent known for her
coverage of the Greek Civil War from 1946 to 1949; and

Ann Beckmann (1972-1978), a reporter for the Madison
Capital Times until an October 1977 strike. Women
were also involved in the field of editing. Civil
rights activist Anne Braden was the education editor
for the Louisville Times and with her husband, Carl,
served as co-editor of The Southern Patriot, the
Southern Conference Education Fund (SCEF) newspaper.
Likewise Edith Isaacs' papers (1889-1957) reflect her
work as a journalist and editor. Her magazine,
Theatre Arts, published some of the earliest works of
Eugene O'Neill, Thornton Wilder, William Saroyan, and
Paul Green and helped to advance the careers of drama
critics and scenic designers as well.

Women have also made inroads into the field of
broadcasting. Newton Minow's papers include a tape
recording of his 1961 speech to the Overseas Press
Club in which he discusses women in television news.
The papers (1906-1962) of Alice Keith reflect the
work of a pioneer in educational broadcasting and
founder and director of the National Academy of
Broadcasting. The Aline Hazard papers (1938-1965)
contain files for The Homemakers Program, a WHA-radio
show for which Hazard served as announcer and later
director. In addition to documenting Hazard's career,
the files provide information about the type of programming that was specifically aimed at women. Further information on programming can be found in the
records of WHA Radio (1968-1974) and WHA Television
(1950-1977), both Madison-based educational stations,
and the records (1920-1969) of the National Broadcasting Company (NBC). The latter collection consists of scripts, programming files, and office files
and provides a good overview of the network's operation from the 1930's through the 1950's. It reveals
the network's attempt to design programming specifically for women and includes the files of Berta
Brainard, who was in charge of the women's programming
department and papers of Barbara Ann, who was responsible for religious programming. NBC's radio and
television scripts also provide a rich source for

women's studies as both are powerful mass media. The image of women which they portrayed helped reinforce or dispel stereotypes and gave their women audiences role models after which to pattern their lives.

Advertising collections also provide useful information, as many of the advertising campaigns were designed specifically to appeal to women. Records (1949-1976) of the Public Relations Society of America include presentations of advertising campaigns from several major agencies on a host of issues and topics. A study of how campaigns were either subtly or overtly geared to women, or of how products designed for women were advertised, would be suitable topics for research. The records (1912-1955) of the Advertising Women of New York, a professional and service organization founded in 1912, include surveys of job opportunities for women from 1942 to 1955, a period when many men were withdrawn from the work force and then re-entered it. The papers (1907-1959) of Dorothy Dignam, one of the first women in advertising and a specialist in advertising women's products and campaigns directed toward women, include extensive samples of her work. The papers (1905-1946) of Alfred Wallace Meyer, another advertising executive, include his campaigns for the first Kotex advertisements. (His first design was rejected because a man appeared too prominently in the advertisement for such a personal product.) A comparison of Dignam's and Meyer's presentations is a likely research undertaking.

Wisconsin Manuscripts

In addition to these special collecting areas, the Society preserves general Wisconsin manuscripts documenting all facets of the state's history. Their broader focus and the fact that they often pre-date the predominantly twentieth century records that are typical of the other collecting areas make the general Wisconsin collections a rich source for women's studies. Often these records portray women whose lives are not individually noteworthy but rather serve as representatives of broad, historic social movements or events. For example, descriptions of immigration and the effects of migration on individuals and families can be located in several small collections. The diary (1852) of Isabella McKinnon recounts her family's journey from Findhorn, Scotland, to Otsego, Wisconsin. In her autobiography (1924) Anna Dicke recalls her childhood and education in Eschenbach, Germany, and her 1849 immigration to America. The papers (1848-1879) of Emma Gattiker trace the movements of three generations of Swiss immigrants who eventually settled in Wisconsin. A brief series of Mrs. M. P. Fishburn's recollections (1845-   ?) describe her childhood and her family's migration from Ohio to Iowa in the mid-1840's. In addition, the papers (1791-1884) of Fritz and Mathilde Franziska Anneke, the latter of whom was a well-known political activist, champion of women's rights, and writer, include exchanges of letters during the couple's period of emigration from Germany following the German Revolution, and their eventual resettlement in America.

Among the holdings of the Wisconsin Jewish Archives, a special collection within the Archives Division about Jewish individuals and organizations relating to Wisconsin, are several oral history interviews in which Jewish women recount their immigration to the United States. Among these are Ida Berkowitz (1954), a Kenosha woman who emigrated from Poland with her parents in 1906; Clara Brown (1954), a Milwaukee resident who emigrated from Russia in 1882 and who describes Jewish community life in both Russia and Milwaukee; and Bertha Langer Raymond (1954), a Jewish woman who emigrated from Prague, Czechoslovakia, and who comments upon her life in Chicago, Detroit, and Milwaukee. With these interviews researchers may compare Jewish life in several urban centers and study the changes that occurred in the attitudes, beliefs, and life styles of the general Jewish community and of individual families as a result of their move to the

United States.

Another approach to women's papers in the general Wisconsin collections is to concentrate on fields or professions in which women were traditionally more active, for example, education and health care. (Public records of course supplement these private manuscript collections.) Several collections document women's involvement in education as students, teachers, and administrators. Ida Bliss's diaries, being a portion of the M. N. Bliss Family diaries (1867-1888), describe both her school and social life. Recollections (1940) of Edna Chynoweth recall her student life in the late 1860's, and letters (1848-1879) of Anna Gattiker detail her student days at the University of Wisconsin from 1875 to 1879. Diaries (1893-1950) of Prairie du Sac resident Louise Bailey document her life as a student at Whitewater Normal School from 1898 to 1900 and later as a teacher in Wisconsin and Minnesota. Other teachers' papers include Ruth Isham's correspondence (1880-1884, 1897-1900), which focuses on her four years as a school teacher in Argentina; Saide Cresswell's reminiscences (1955), which recall her experiences as a teacher in North Dakota around 1900; and the papers (1881-1950) of Nellie Kedzie Jones, which document the life of a pioneer educator in the field of college home economics. In addition to the records of students and teachers, the Charles Crownhart Family papers (1862-1943) include those of his wife Jessie, who was a superintendent of schools in Douglas County and a member of the Board of Regents of the Normal School. An organizational perspective of women educators and education may be found in the records (1852-1964) of Milwaukee-Downer College, formed by the merger of two women's schools, the records (1927-1972) of the Wisconsin Division of the American Association of University Women, and the records (1923-1943) of the Wisconsin section of the National Council of Administrative Women in Education.

Health care also has been a major interest of women

through the years. The activities of nurses can be seen in the diaries (1861-1863) of Emilie C. Quiner, a Civil War nurse in a Union hospital in Memphis, and in the letters (1918) of Margaret Rowland, a Red Cross nurse in a French hospital during World War I. The training and increasing professionalization of these women may be traced in the records (1894-1972) of Milwaukee's St. Mary's School of Nursing, a hospital-organized training school founded by the Sister's of Charity in 1894, which ultimately affiliated with the University of Wisconsin-Milwaukee's degree nursing program. Papers (1919-1972) of nurse and teacher Ethel J. Odegard not only include some of the files of the Milwaukee Central School of Nursing but also reveal her efforts to further the professionalization of nursing by linking hospital nursing schools with colleges and vocational institutions. Records (1919-1950) of the Wisconsin State League of Nursing Education show its attempt to promote uniform standards in nursing education.

Women also became physicians. Although their numbers were comparatively few, the actions of these pioneers reflect the intent of women to participate at every level of the medical profession. One example is the papers (1945-1962) of Kate Newcomb, a Woodruff, Wisconsin, physician who struggled to organize and build the Lakeland Memorial Hospital. Another, Dr. Elizabeth Comstock, practiced in Arcadia after training in New York and is represented in an extensive family collection. The collection was used by Merle E. Curti in his volume on Trempealeau County, Wisconsin, entitled The Making of an American Community: A Case Study of Democracy in a Frontier County (1959). Women's health concerns are also reflected in the records (1898-1960) of the Attic Angel Association, a Madison-based philanthropic organization which, beginning in 1908, sponsored and sustained the city's first visiting nurse program.

Descriptions of the daily lives of all classes of women abound in the general Wisconsin collections.

Sarah Fairchild's correspondence in the Lucius Fairchild papers (1826-1923) describes the lives of women in both Madison and Superior. Annie Gorham Marston's diaries, located in the James W. Gorham papers, record household life on a farm and Madison social events. Two diaries (1847-1854) of Caroline Greenman detail the daily life, work, and social activities of a single girl in Massachusetts. Martha Gunnison's diaries (1879-1957) chronicle the life of a housewife in Waupun, Wisconsin, and Detroit, Michigan. The Henry S. Baird papers (1798-1937) include those of his wife Elizabeth which depict frontier life in Green Bay and the political and social changes the community underwent as it became more densely populated. Numerous letters by female members of the Lawe, Grignon, and Boyd families which appear in the respective family collections are another source for women in early Wisconsin. Diaries kept by Jane Bewell Kelly (1866-1898) mirror the daily life of a mother and later grandmother of a large family in a deeply religious rural community. Diary entries of Helen Barstow (1851, 1854, 1856) concern domestic, social, and local events in Waukesha, while those of Maria Merrill (1890-1899) deal with family and household affairs and the operation of their farm in Sechlerville. Farm life is further documented in several oral history interviews with Lois Linse Gleiter (1974), Jean Stillman Long (1974), and Margaret Segerstrom (1976).

The Society also has two other major collections in which materials on women can be found--the McCormick Collection and the Draper Manuscripts. Detailed guides to both collections (<u>Guide to the McCormick Collection of the State Historical Society of Wisconsin</u> and a forthcoming guide to the Draper Manuscripts) describe the holdings and provide insight into women's lives from the eighteenth through the twentieth centuries.

Draper and McCormick Manuscripts

For more than thirty years Lyman C. Draper served as corresponding secretary of the State Historical Society of Wisconsin. His private research collection (1740-1891), comprising nearly 500 volumes, reflects his interest in the history of the trans-Allegheny West, from the Indian wars of the 1740's through the War of 1812. Although the amount of material by or pertaining to women is comparatively sparse and scattered throughout the collection, interesting references can be found by the persistent researcher.

As a historical and biographical researcher and avid collector of manuscripts, Draper was interested in women as individuals only if they had played some role in the settlement process or military events he hoped to chronicle or in the lives of frontiersmen whose biographies he intended to write. Thus, the collection includes letters and articles detailing the bravery of Elizabeth Zane during the 1782 siege of Wheeling, the activities of Carolinian Whig women who warned of impending Tory attacks during the Revolution, and the plight of frontier women in Indian raids and captivities. A few of the original manuscripts Draper collected were written by or to eighteenth-century women. Among these are various business and legal documents signed by women and occasional personal letters such as those written by William Harrod and William Patterson to their wives and by Anne Christian to her husband. The collection includes summaries of approximately 1,200 interviews and conversations of which about 230 were with women. In the Kentucky papers (Series CC) the interviews recorded by John Shane, Presbyterian minister and historian, provide greater insights into frontier social and economic conditions than Draper's own notes. In providing accounts of their daily lives, the women whom Shane interviewed described the hardships of crossing mountains, their sadness over the abandonment of treasured possessions, and their pleasure in social gatherings such as weddings and dances. Some recalled household chores such as making sugar and salt or weaving cloth from nettles and buffalo wool.

Interview notes include recollections from at least three black women: "Aunt Phyllis," daughter of an African black who had participated in the Revolution in South Carolina; "Aunt Polly," a former slave of the Thomas Sumter family; and Rachel Johnson, a survivor of the 1779 and 1782 Indian sieges at Wheeling. More extensive references on Native American women appear, since Draper gathered data on the influence of a few individual women such as the Cherokee, Nancy Ward, and Molly Brant, sister of the Mohawk leader Joseph Brant. Descriptions of the conditions of life and tribal status of Native American women are also recounted in the writings of two Indian agents, John Johnston and Thomas Forsyth.

A new guide to the entire Draper Manuscripts and a microfilm edition of the calendars for nine of the larger series of volumes are in preparation. In addition all of the Draper Manuscripts are available on microfilm.

The McCormick Collection consists of a series of papers of individuals, companies, and organizations associated with the life and work of Cyrus McCormick, inventor of the reaper. Among the individuals are two prominent women--Nettie Fowler McCormick, the inventor's wife, and Anita McCormick Blaine, one of their daughters.

The papers (1775-1949, 1962) of Nettie Fowler McCormick consist of correspondence, legal documents, financial files, and volumes of diaries, memorabilia, and scrapbooks which reveal her family, business, and philanthropic affairs. She regularly corresponded with her children, and with those charged with their care during separations. The family's domestic accounts are contained in a series of bills, receipts, and statements and show the life style of a wealthy family. Her business acumen was recognized and appreciated by both her husband and later her son, who ran the family firm. As their counselor, advisor, and aide, she was fully conversant with the operation of the McCormick Harvesting Machine Company. Frequent letters with family members and company officials focus on business affairs. After her husband's death and once the firm was firmly under her son's control, she devoted more of her time to a host of philanthropic causes in which she was deeply interested. Her papers reveal her personal and financial support of organizations that embodied the concept of Christian service, such as the McCormick Theological Seminary, and a host of small schools and academies that stressed self-help and manual training for students. She was also interested in the plight of those living in southern Appalachia and assisted the Home Industrial School at Asheville, North Carolina, the Laurel Schools, and projects in mountain crafts. Among other organizations and causes to which McCormick lent her support were several Chicago-area groups such as Hull House, Juvenile Protection Association, Women's Christian Temperance Union, and the University of Chicago Settlement, the Presbyterian Church and its various missions and boards of education, the Young Men's Christian Association, the Young Women's Christian Association, and many foreign mission schools.

The papers (1828-1958) of Anita McCormick Blaine consist of correspondence, reports, diaries, speeches, writings, financial documents, and records relating to personal expenditures and the operation of her household and office. They concern not only her family and personal business affairs, but also focus on her wide-ranging personal and philanthropic interests such as education, child welfare, social reform, world peace, and international cooperation. A supporter of Francis W. Parker, she contributed to experimental education projects. Among these was the Chicago Institute, which ultimately formed the University of Chicago's School of Education. Other examples of her

interests in education were her establishment of the Francis W. Parker Elementary School on Chicago's near north side for the benefit of low-income families and her membership on the city's board of education.
After World War I, world peace and international understanding absorbed more of her energies, as she was interested in both the League of Nations and later the United Nations. Extensive documentation also exists for the World Citizen Association, organized in 1938 in Anita's home and designed to research and publicize the need for world cooperation. Materials also relate to the Pocono Peace Conference which she helped plan and finance and which discussed extragovernmental means to resolve international differences.

Public Records

Public records produced by state, county, and local governments are another rich source of historical information. As government hires and fires, performs social services, regulates, legislates, and adjudicates, it affects the lives of all its citizens--including women--and these activities are part of the public record.

The state archives consist of records created by the legislative, executive, and judicial branches of Wisconsin as each performs its authorized functions--to determine the state's policies and programs, to carry out these programs, and to determine the limits of governmental power and the extent of individual rights. Many of the state's activities designed to fulfill these functions are of potential interest to students of women's history, such as its concern with health care, education, crime control, and human relations and resources. Records to document these and other activities may be found in the state archives and are filed by the agency which originally created or assembled the materials.

For example, Bureau of Personnel files are located

among the records of the Department of Administration. A rudimentary knowledge of the state's organization and functions (which may be gleaned from the Wisconsin Blue Book, published biennially) or the assistance of the reference archivists will make the seeming labyrinth of public records more understandable. The following section suggests some individual series or record groups (i.e., groupings of several series) which contain relevant materials for women's studies.

   Wisconsin engages in the collective bargaining process both by negotiating with its own employees and by acting as a mediator between private management and labor unions. A study of the Bureau of Personnel files would reveal the state's attitude toward its women employees, while the Employment Relations Board files might provide some additional insights into the working woman's plight in the private sector. The state's involvement in public health care provides sources for studying the commitment and treatment of women patients in mental hospitals. For example, State Board of Control records include the files of the superintendent of the Mendota Hospital for the Insane that contain information on the home's operation. Additional records relating to the care and condition of Mendota's patients may be found in the files of the Public Welfare Department. Executive files include materials from the Governor's Employment Relations Study Committee (1976-1977) and from the defunct Governor's Commission on the Status of Women, the latter group charged with investigating the conditions and quality of life of Wisconsin women. Records (1946-   ) of the Cosmetology subdivision of the Board of Health consist of reports and correspondence with beauty schools regarding students, curricula, and the requirements for licensing beauty operators in Wisconsin. For Health Education (1940-1953) the Board of Health's files include correspondence, schedules of lectures, reports, replies to questionnaires and descriptions of high school sex education programs; for Maternity Hospitals (1929-   )

the Board of Health preserved correspondence and reports relating to their licensing. Records of the State Historical Society of Wisconsin document the work of female librarians, archivists, curators, and historians whose efforts helped to establish the Society's national reputation. Department of Justice files include 1973 correspondence from concerned citizens regarding the U.S. Supreme Court's decision on abortion. The Board of Medical Examiners records include applicant files (1909-1934) from individuals seeking licenses as midwives. Records of the Department of Nurses include correspondence, course outlines, and examinations from nursing schools and dossiers on nurses. Records of the State Department of Public Welfare's Division of Corrections contain files relating to the Wisconsin School for Girls and the Wisconsin Home for Women; records of its Division of Children and Youth, Community Services Subdivision, include administrative files from the biennial Governor's Conference on Children and Youth. Among the Public Assistance files of the Department of Public Welfare are Transient Family Case Records (1933-1937). Records of the State Board of Education might also prove useful.

County and local records may include records produced by the register of deeds, county clerk, superintendent of schools, treasurer, the courts, and the police department. Social welfare, local government and politics, and education are a few of the subjects that hold particular relevance for women's history. Prior to the federal government's assumption of aid programs in the 1930's, social welfare assistance fell to county and local governments. Many of their records concern aid to dependent children, widow's pensions, and health care services, all subjects of particular interest to women. Records of mental health institutions, such as county homes and mental hospitals, provide information on the commitment and treatment of women, both as individuals and in the aggregate. Court records, including both circuit and county courts, contain divorce and probate records and the records relating to the convictions of prostitutes, as well as scores of other court cases involving women. Tax rolls, when used with plat books, provide a source for documenting individual women as property holders and thus help to evaluate their role in the economy. School district and county superintendents' records are other significant primary sources of information since women constitute a high proportion of teachers and a few even held elective school offices before passage of the suffrage act. These records would illustrate their work conditions and career patterns. Similarly, records of county teacher colleges document institutions whose student bodies were almost exclusively female.

Specific examples of relevant county and local records include a Criminal Docket (1887-1897) from Lincoln County's Clerk of Municipal Court, which records prostitution charges; Contracts Salary Lists and Salary Schedules (1913-1958) from Rock County, which lists teachers' names and salaries and general salary schedules for various levels of training and experience; Register of Births (1854-1911) from Milwaukee County's Register of Deeds which includes information on illegitimate births and stillbirths; the Register of Sporting People (1900-1910) is a record of prostitutes registered by the city of Superior's Police Department; the Mother's Pension Payment Register (1931-1934) from Brown County's treasurer; the Police Women's Daily Report (1954-   ) from the City of Kenosha's Police Department, which logs activities and cases that concern topics such as child neglect and abuse, women, and family troubles; Registration of Marriages (1844-1896) from Portage County's Register of Deeds; Midwives and Physician's Reports (1888-1903) from Pierce County's Register of Deeds; Record of Registered Nurses (1913) from Ashland County's Clerk; County Nurse Files (1920-1924) from Price County's Department of Public Welfare which relate to cases such as unwed mothers and illegitimate, neglected and abused children; and the John H. Palmeter's Old Ladies Home Records (1898-1942) from the Clerk of Circuit Court of Racine County.

The Society's efforts to collect and preserve the record of our past have resulted in massive holdings of both public and private records. Through the years, this active collecting policy has neither consciously nor unconsciously excluded women's papers; consequently, the holdings of the Archives Division today contain some of the richest source material in the United States for the study of women. They document women's participation in all facets of American life--as housewives, pacifists, nurses, economic theoreticians, actresses, teachers, dramatists, administrators, civil rights workers, executives, and anonymous individuals. This section has attempted to describe a few of these sources and to give some indication of their variety and potential uses. It is hoped that this effort will encourage researchers to come to the Archives and use these records. For it is only with their use that women's contributions to American society will be fully revealed.

ICONOGRAPHIC COLLECTIONS

The Iconographic Collections constitute part of the Visual and Sound Collections of the Archives Division. The present collection dates from the reorganization of the picture files in 1954 when Paul Vanderbilt was hired as Curator. The files encompass a vast conglomeration of photographs, lithographs, paintings, drawings, posters, cartoons, postcards, lantern slides, magazine clippings and advertisements, motion pictures, and other graphic ephemera including broadsides, greeting cards, trade catalogs, dance programs, letterheads, business cards, and so forth. Numbering well over one million items, the collection is oriented towards inquiry in the fields of folklore and folklife, social history, anthropology, sociology, and economics. The filing systems reveal the true essence of Iconography, namely, "the collecting of a quantity of representations of the same or related subjects with a view to comparative study."

Access to the collection is through three self-organizing files as well as more traditional archival approaches.

A Portrait or Name File includes formal views of individuals and corporate groups, and files them by alphabetic sub-groups, e.g., the surname Bonner is filed with surnames Bol-Bon; but Carrie Jacobs Bond is singled out for special treatment in a separate folder.

The geographic Place File contains individually mounted images including land, city, and townscapes, building views and other aspects of the built environment to facilitate the comparative study of a place over time.

A third self-organizing file is the General Subject Classification scheme originally designed by Paul Vanderbilt in Philadelphia and applied to the photographic output of the Farm Security Administration housed at the Library of Congress. Redesigned to take existing strengths and needs into account, the Society's file consists of topically arranged groups of picture portfolios within a classified subject arrangement. The general outline encompasses sixteen major headings: land; cities; people; homes and living conditions; transportation; work; process and manufacturing; selling and distribution; services; organized society; war and military affairs; medicine; religion; intellectual and creative activity; social and personal activity; recreation; dissipation and crime. Within each group the heading is defined more specifically. For example, under the section on "Process and Manufacturing" the following subsections are enumerated:

Manufacturing	Ceramics, Clay Products,
Food Production	Tile Pottery
Dairy Products	Brickmaking
Grist Mills	Glassware Manufacture
Brewing Industry	Metals Production
Leather	Machine Shops
Textile Manufacture	Machinery Manufacture
Clothing Industry	Agricultural Machinery Manu-
Wood Products	facture
Charcoal	Jewelry, Gems, etc., Pro-
Paper and Pulp Mills	cessing
Container Industry	Carriage and Wagon Making
Printing	Automotive Manufacturing
Petroleum Products	Shipbuilding
Stone and Stone Products	
Cement, Lime, and Related Products	

The bulk of the collection is contained in archival lots, units or group entries described on catalog cards and extensively cross-referenced throughout alphabetical subject headings. Albums, scrapbooks, family picture collections, photographers, accumulated prints and negatives, and many other items are treated in this manner.

An additional filing system includes individual oversize items, historic prints, posters and broadsides, but reference prints are also filed in the appropriate locations within the other filing systems.

While there are specific subject headings applicable to a study of women's history, such as "Women's Suffrage," it is important to remember that in order to gain a comprehensive understanding of women through visual resources, a researcher should be prepared to be flexible in approach and imaginative in the choice of headings pursued. As with any serious research project, researchers also must be prepared to examine a quantity of pictures in various files. Women appear almost as frequently as men, yet they are not always central to the photographers' intent. Close attention must be paid to the subtleties involved in the picture-taking process if the lives of women, especially those whose lives passed unnoticed in the public's eye, are to be studied.

A strength of the Society's collections is the documentation of family life, particularly in small towns at the turn of the century. Subject headings of particular importance for researchers studying family history or mother-child and mother-father role relationships would include "home life," "family," and "mothers and adults with children." An exceptional view of the private life of public figures Robert M. and Belle Case La Follette is found in the family album assembled by Isabel Bacon La Follette which records a charming portrait of home life and children including Fola, Mary, Bob, Jr., Phil, and a dog named "Bud," picnicking, play-acting, and gardening--all depicted without pretension. The work of such amateur photographers as Francis M. Meinhardt, Frederick King Conover, Herman Taylor, Harry E. Dankoler, and Edward Bass portray the intimacy embedded within the traditional family structure. The collections of Andrew Dahl and Charles Van Schaick offer many views of family groups in south-central Wisconsin from 1871-1879 and Black River Falls, Wisconsin, from 1890-1910 respectively, and their more formal portrayal expands the vision gained from the personal collections already mentioned. Mothers, female children, female hired help, and female relatives appear simultaneously in carefully ordered settings indicative of a certain hierarchy.

An extension of family life materials is the wide range of items covering children and young adults. Children can be found in school, out of school, at work, at play, with adults and with pets, in formal portrait photos, and so forth. All of these provide an excellent source for the study of children's development in nineteenth and early twentieth-century America. A series of photographs dealing with the Hillside Home School operated by Misses Ellen and Jane Lloyd-Jones, a Unitarian-influenced progressive school, documents just such role-modeling. Young girls are learning to cook and to sew, in this case, alongside young boys. Other collections on the Wisconsin Industrial School for Girls, the agricultural service extension classes of the University of Wisconsin, and private finishing schools illustrate the emphasis on domestic science. Another source for study is the scrapbooks, dance books, and albums assembled by young ladies of means. Rebecca P. Flint's are typical of an age in which young women carefully hoarded party mementoes and dance cards and all manner of personal memorabilia and ephemera. A study of Rebecca's scrapbook during the time (1915-1916) she was abroad tutoring the children of Ambassador to Norway, Alfred G. Schmedemann, would tell us a great deal about the social interactions of an American abroad.

The family material, while certainly substantial, is but a fraction of the relevant material available for study. It is important for the researcher to move beyond the obvious traditional family and work roles such as teaching and nursing. When one examines a large number of photographs of lumber camps in northern Wisconsin, the obvious male-dominance of the scene is modified by the significant number of women. Women worked in the camps, sharing the same rugged existence of the men as wives, mothers, mothers-to-be, cooks, cook's helpers, and bookkeepers. (They also visited the camps frequently.) This same phenomenon can be observed in other occupational and industrial settings including the clothing industry, tanning, tobacco, newspaper typesetting, merchandising, and cigar manufacturing, to name but a few. Researchers easily can examine large segments of the collection, a fact which makes such sweeps more practical. <u>Milwaukee Journal</u> newsphotos introduce work roles pursued by women in the recent past.

Much of the Iconographic Collections augment related manuscript holdings and focus both on the personal and professional lives of such women as Zona Gale (author and playwright), Ada James and Carrie Chapman Catt (suffragists), Alice and Bettina Jackson (Madison social reformers), Anita McCormick Blaine (philanthropist), and Dickey Chapelle (reporter/photographer). While it is easier to focus on these known women, it is also possible to search the files systematically for the ordinary women among portraits of husbands and families.

Among other topics which might be pursued is that of women artists or of women as portrayed in the graphic arts. Although not a fine arts collection, the Iconographic Collections do contain some original watercolors, woodcuts, sketches, and drawings retained as being valid for their subject matter interest. For the most part these are by regional artists, including Marie Bleck of Oshkosh, who was involved in the Wisconsin Federal Art Project during the 1930's, Emma

Glenz, an artist with the Wisconsin State Highway Commission, and Dorothy Meeker and Winifred Ford of Madison. There is much more material available in the graphic arts for the study of how women have been portrayed at various time periods. An extensive collection of chromolithographic trade cards and advertising ephemera illustrates early versions of the "pin-up" girl. Wood engravings from the popular press of the late nineteenth century contain sentimental renderings of home life and the woman as "ministering angel." Posters from both world wars afford an opportunity to study artists' conceptions of women and include such examples from the standard repertoire as "ministering wife," symbol of liberty, "the Mother of us all," the long-suffering widow, and military-approved "pin-ups." These symbols helped to advise both the civilian and military populace about government-encouraged standards of behavior. Beyond the material issued by the U.S. Food Administration and the U.S. Office of War Information, there are Red Cross and United War Work Campaign posters illustrating another aspect of civilian participation in wartime activities.

Most of the specific interest shown in women as photographers has centered on women who have achieved prominence on the national and international scene: Imogen Cunningham, Diane Arbus, Bernice Abbott, Julia Margaret Cameron, and Frances Benjamin Johnston. The Society does not have in its collections photographic prints by any of these women. The material available to the researcher centers on women as amateur photographers, and includes the work of Annie Sievers Schildhauer, the wife of a Wisconsin civil servant who directed the lens of her camera at the houses of friends and at the details of homelife in the 1890's. Her talents included both photography and painting. Grace Gilbert Viel photographed her family and the town of New London, Wisconsin; her negatives were a gift from her niece Neita Oviatt Friend, who herself began taking pictures with a postcard camera during her last years at Milwaukee-Downer Seminary. An intriguing album of photoprints undoubtedly taken by a woman (a self-portrait appears taken in a mirrored reflection) came with the estate of Valentine Krueger of Horicon, Wisconsin. A collection which is known and has recently become more complete is the Blanchard Harper negatives. Harper apparently was commissioned to do architectural studies for the University and the Historical Society around 1900, and her material was used to illustrate the dedicatory volume about the Society's building. Other images in her collection include many scenic views of the Turville Point landscape in Madison and the Turville and Thwaites families. Meticulously maintained records of exposure and time of shooting indicate more than a passing fancy on her part. Why Blanchard Harper did not continue to shoot after this time period remains a mystery, as her family's descendants remember her only as a musician and piano teacher.

Many other women were active in commercial photography, and the Directory of Wisconsin Photographers, an ongoing effort to identify all commercial photographers in Wisconsin from the 1840's through the end of World War I, is a systematic effort which will help to document this group. The project has brought to light the contributions of female daguerreotypists, photographers, photo-finishers, photo-retouchers, colorists and tinters, and apprentice technicians as well as managers of photographic studios and supply stores, checkers, clerks, bookkeepers, and receptionists. This is primarily raw data; much research needs to be done before we have a fuller view and understanding of such women as the Clizbe Sisters of Sauk City, Ella Buck of Fort Atkinson, and Marcella Brown of La Crosse. To date approximately 2,000 names have been recorded of Wisconsin women in photography, and as the project continues more will certainly be discovered about some of the women who became involved in photography through their own initiative as well as through the circumstances of inheritance and widowhood.

The Iconographic Collections Study Room is open to researchers from 8 to 5, Monday through Friday. The collections are non-circulating but material can be copied in several ways: Xerox and continuous-tone same-size copies which are suitable as reference prints can be made in-house; photographic enlargement prints suitable for publication (a fee schedule is available on request); or 35mm color or black-and-white slides for projection uses can be ordered with a time lag of two to three weeks. Patrons are allowed to make their own color copy slides on the premises if previous arrangements have been made with the Reference Assistant. Appointments to reserve the copystand area should be made by calling (608) 262-9581.

There is no published catalogue to the holdings. Patrons unable to visit the Collections to examine the files are encouraged to review this statement of collection organization so as to better understand the kinds of material found within the confines of the section's collecting areas. The following is a selected list of publications which contain reproduced images from the Society's Iconographic Collections: Jensen, Oliver, American Album, 1968; Lesy, Michael, Wisconsin Death Trip, 1973; Nesbit, Robert, Wisconsin: A History, 1973; Norfleet, Barbara, Wedding, 1979; Sear, Stephen, Hometown U.S.A., 1975; Szarkowski, John, The Photographer's Eye, 1966; Talbot, George, At Home: Domestic Life in the Post-Centennial Era 1876-1920, 1976; Time-Life, This Fabulous Century; Wisconsin: Portrait of the Past; A Photographic Journey Through Wisconsin, Vols. I and II, 1971 and 1972; and the Wisconsin Magazine of History.

Mary Tyler Moore, Betty White, and Gavin McLeod in the WJM-TV newsroom of "The Mary Tyler Moore Show," CBS, c. 1975. [Wisconsin Center for Film and Theater Research, negative no. 4758]

Assembly line at Nash (later American) Motors, Kenosha, c. 1917. [Women's Committee, State Council of Defense, Madison, WHi (X3) 15456]

In 1910, when William A. Titus took this photo of Marcella Maude Sievers, she was employed in his company, Standard Lime & Stone of Fond du Lac. Her successive careers as stenographer, cashier, and bookkeeper ended with her marriage to Guy E. More in 1917. [WHi (T57) 41]

Residential neighborhood, Los Angeles, 1946. [Lloyd Barbee collection, WHi (X3) 35376]

Alex Lonetree, his wife and daughter, John Hazen Hill ("Red Bill"), and Wolf Woman (seated right), photographed around the turn of the century by Charles Van Schaick of Black River Falls. [WHi (V24) 2003]

Bridal shower, 1957. [Photograph by Richard Vesey of the Wisconsin State Journal, Madison, Iconographic Collections Lot 3365 / no. 117]

Greyhound Bus stop, Main Street, Marshall, 1961. [Photograph by Richard Vesey, Iconographic Collections Lot 3365 / no. 567]

Milwaukee nurses, c. 1914. [Photographed by J. Robert Taylor of the Milwaukee Journal, WHi (X3) 19848]

Poster, Vietnam war.
[WHi (X3) 37873]

Poster, World War I.
[WHi (X3) 37689]

The screenplay for "Beyond the Forest" (Warner Brothers, 1949) was written by Lenore J. Coffee. [Wisconsin Center for Film and Theater Research, United Artists Series 1.5]

Edith Head's costume renderings for "Sex and the Single Girl" (Warner Brothers, 1964).
[WHi (X3) 35379]

Dressing up, 1962. [Photographed by Richard Vesey, Iconographic Collections Lot 3365 / no. 713]

Nancy Kaye Trewyn of Whitewater, the "Alice" of 1957 in a contest sponsored since 1948 by the Marketing Division of the Wisconsin Department of Agriculture, Trade and Consumer Protection. [WHI (X3) 37750]

Daguerreotype portrait of Rachel Lawe Grignon, daughter of the Green Bay fur trader John Lawe and a Chippewa woman. [WHi (X3) 24634]

Sweet corn line at the Fall River Canning Company, Markesan, c. 1975. [Photographed by L. Roger Turner, WHi (X3) 31908]

Shirley Clarke directing her film "Bullfight" (Halcyon Films, 1955). [Wisconsin Center for Film and Theater Research, negative no. 4767]

Mrs. Ernest G. Kern of Monroe, 1956. [Photographed by Richard Vesey, Iconographic Collections, Lot 3365 / no. 46]

Katharine Hepburn in "Christopher Strong," an RKO movie of 1933 directed by Dorothy Arzner. [Wisconsin Center for Film and Theater Research, Negative no. 519]

From "Elizabeth Harding, Bride," a promotional pamphlet distributed by Ivory Soap, c. 1910. [WHi (X3) 35379]

Wedding portrait by Charles Van Schaick of Black River Falls, c. 1890. [WHi (V22) 1301]

THE MUSEUM

Several areas of the Society's Museum will aid researchers interested in women's history: fine arts, decorative or home arts, and family life. Home arts, such as weaving and quilting, were important to women in the nineteenth and twentieth centuries. Whether functional results were in mind or not, such work was (and is) a creative outlet. Wealthy women did not have an exclusive hold on non-functional creations, for to make something for sheer creative joy, or sense of accomplishment and decorative impact, is a universal impulse. One example of this would be the chamber pot covers in the Society's collections. In addition to examples of weaving and quilting the Museum has lace bobbins, lacemaker's reels, looms, spinning wheels, yarn winders, thimbles, needlecases, pincushions, and a wealth of ephemera related to tatting, netting, crocheting, beading, and embroidery.
 Many women's practical and artistic creations have substantial esthetic merit, but, because of social pressures or norms, the works seldom reached the marketplace, aside from the garments made by seamstresses who went from house to house, annually sewing clothing for women and children in a family. Nonetheless, some Wisconsin women became renowned serious artists in their day, especially the sculptors Vinnie Ream Hoxie, Jean Miner, and Helen Farnsworth Mears. Susan Porter Green's biography <u>Helen Farnsworth Mears</u> (1972) provides one of the most comprehensive accounts of a woman artist available. Two women who specialized in art pottery, Pauline

Jacobus of Edgerton and Susan Frackelton of Milwaukee, achieved commercial success and were inspirations to the hundreds of amateur potters, china painters, and decorators who thrived in Wisconsin in the late nineteenth and early twentieth centuries. Jacobus' Pauline ware was cast from molds designed by herself and others working in her shop as was the underglaze decoration. Frackelton earned her lasting reputation in the hand-formed Milwaukee clay art wares which she created and exhibited all over the world. The Society's Museum possesses many examples of both women's work. Further documentation of Frackelton's career is found in George Weedon's <u>Susan S. Frackelton and the American Arts and Crafts Movement</u> (1975); Jacobus' work is represented in a slide series in the Museum's files.

The women's clothing collection can serve as a barometer to study obvious manifestations of changing social values and positions of women in society. The trend from the confining, yet voluminous clothing of the nineteenth century in part reflects the liberation of women that continues into the present. For example, undergarments, the armor and guard of ladylike femininity, evolved slowly into nothingness by the 1930's. The specialization of clothing for sports, leisure, and work is documented in the collection, with dual purpose of tracing the changing industrial economy and the relative position of women in society--the alteration from a polite, genteel, idleness to twentiety-century freedom.

Some authorities consider the Museum's collection of garments from 1830 to the 1960's to be well documented, particularly from 1830 to the 1890's. The Society sponsors "Patterns of History," an ongoing project to produce patterns of women's dresses at decennial intervals from 1835 to 1899. The Patterns project is unique for two reasons: the styles are accurately drafted from original nineteenth-century dresses (a procedure not done elsewhere for public distribution) and the costumes chosen for reproduction are not the elaborate creations made for wealthy women, but instead reflect ordinary middle-class everyday dress. It is possible partially to define the role of ethnic women from the collections, though not for every nationality. For women who immigrated early or were insular enough to maintain some Old World crafts and customs, the tracing can be completed more accurately. Much of the Society's collection is now on loan to Old World Wisconsin, the Society's outdoor ethnic museum in Eagle.

Household furnishings and appliances aid in gaining a perspective on life over the last 150 years. The Society's holdings especially reveal aspects of middle-class life styles. The documentation of post-pioneer settlement by the working classes--farmers and laborers, both blue and white collar--is less complete. Overall, the collection contains a large and inclusive selection of English ceramics of the late eighteenth through the late nineteenth centuries of the kind used in every home. The representative collection of American glass is mostly of the pressed variety. The Museum's holdings of American crockery used in early homes, especially early Wisconsin earthenware and salt glazed ware, give telling evidence of various life styles. Kitchen and dairy equipment for the home complete the picture. Dolls and other toys provide researchers with a veriety of images that can be used to reveal sex and class structure. Fine ornamental French, Chinese, and Dresden wares from upper-class families plus oriental rugs, elaborate furnishings and lighting devices, and fine tableware and linens all aid in drawing comparisons that frequently parallel those drawn from the study of clothing.

The Museum has a small but excellent library on these art forms, including books and periodicals. Study facilities are available on consultation with the Museum Director and appropriate curators by appointment.

FILM ARCHIVE, WISCONSIN CENTER FOR FILM AND THEATER RESEARCH

The Wisconsin Center for Film and Theater Research is a cooperative venture of the University of Wisconsin-Madison and the State Historical Society of Wisconsin. Founded in 1960, the Center now has over 200 film and manuscript collections from motion picture, television, and theatrical directors, actors, writers, producers, and production companies. The Center's Film Archive is located on the fourth floor of the State Historical Society. It has Steenbeck flat-bed viewing machines for individual screening and study of films in the collections. Access to sound and graphic materials relating to the performing arts is also available through the Film Archive. Reference service and access to manuscript materials are available during the Center's regular hours, but viewing time for films and graphics must be reserved in advance.

For researchers interested in the portrayal of women by entertainment media, and the impact that this portrayal has had upon twentieth-century society, the film collections of the WCFTR provide an invaluable resource for first-hand examination of how Hollywood perceived, and purveyed, its women.

The period between 1930 and 1950, extensively documented by the Center's film holdings, is often looked upon as the "Golden Age" of Hollywood. During these years, the genres and conventions which make up the typical Hollywood film were first defined. Considering the popularity of the medium--in the 1930's and

1940's Americans commonly attended several films each week--it is generally conceded that Hollywood feature films had a powerful influence on, as well as being reflective of, the dominant view of American life.

The United Artists Collection, the Center's largest single collection, includes over 1,700 feature films, 1,500 shorts, and 600 cartoons. Films are both sound and silent, black and white and color. The 16mm reference prints represent the work of three major Hollywood studios: Warner Brothers, RKO, and Monogram, from 1918 through 1955. The 180 Monogram titles are typical of small, low-budget productions in the 1930's and 1940's. The 702 RKO titles include nearly all the feature films produced by this major company during the same period. The Warner library, with over 800 features, is unique in that it contains a virtually complete record of the studio's output between 1931 and 1949--hundreds of low-budget pictures as well as more prestigious releases. The comprehensiveness of this library allows the scholar to examine films in relation to a studio's overall style. The way in which the narrative, the characterization, or the technique of a particular film represents the female protagonist can be compared to films of the same year, genre, or level of production. The images used to define women, the behavior expected of them, the cinematography and lighting that were used to portray them, can all be examined in order to determine a specific "Warner's style" of female representation and to compare this style with that of other Hollywood studios.

The Warner library is also rich in manuscript documentation. Film scripts, ranging from original treatments to final shooting scripts, are available on almost every title through the Archives Division Reading Room of the State Historical Society. For example, it is possible to trace the evolution of a film such as <u>Beyond the Forest</u> (1949, Warner Brothers) from a simple story outline, proposed by the author of the novel from which the film was taken, through the six Temporary, Final, and Revised Final scripts written by one of the studio's most active screenwriters, Lenore Coffee. Additional women screenwriters, independents as well as those who were part of the Warner Brothers "stable," were represented in Warner's manuscripts.

The comprehensiveness of the film library also makes it possible to trace the careers of some of film's most powerful and respected actresses: Bette Davis, Joan Crawford, and Katharine Hepburn. Dorothy Arzner, the only woman director in "Golden Age" Hollywood, is also represented in the film holdings by such works as Christopher Strong (1933, RKO) and Dance, Girl, Dance (1940, RKO). The sheer number of films provides an opportunity for statistical analysis of women's on-screen technical credits.

Complementing the United Artists Collection are the 200 titles in the Shepard Collection, which consist of silent films made in the United States and abroad, and later films, most of which were made outside the Hollywood system. The conventions employed by pioneer, foreign, and independent film makers to define their female characters can be examined in relation to those of Hollywood films. Using the Shepard films in conjunction with the United Artists Collection, analyses of change (or lack of it) in cinema's perception and portrayal of the female role can be made following a chronological or cross-cultural model. That is, one can compare the women in a French Impressionist film such as Abel Gance's La Roue (1921) with those in a French New Wave film such as Truffaut's Jules et Jim (1962) or with an early Hollywood film like Ella Cinders (1926, Warner Brothers) or a classic "woman's picture" such as Now, Voyager (1942, Warner Brothers). In addition, the activity of contemporary women film makers is documented in the collections of Perry Miller Adato and Shirley Clarke. The comparisons which can be made through direct observation of the films are limited only by the researcher's imagination and energy.

Since nearly every Hollywood narrative film is based on a male-female relationship, it is difficult to point to material significant to women's history by following traditional subject-cataloging methods. It is perhaps more practical to separate films according to genre, and then, through direct observation of the films of a particular genre, identify the iconographic or structural conventions of that genre that apply to women. Any film's presentation of women can be examined in light of its affirmation of, or departure from, these conventions. A genre listing of most of the Warner Brothers films is available through the Film Archive; such a genre listing for the RKO films is in progress. A Feature Film List, which contains a complete title listing of the films in the United Artists Collection, is available through the Center for $1.00. The Shepard Collection films are indexed by title, each title card containing a brief synopsis which includes genre.

What the Hollywood film was in the 1930's and 1940's, television has been from the 1950's to the present: the most powerful source of entertainment and information for much of the American public. While access to the television programs themselves is a vital element of television research, it is in this area that research has been most difficult. Since it is so difficult for individual scholars to gain access to program materials through the normal channels of distribution, the Center's acquisition of film and video copies of a broad range of television programming is an invaluable resource.

The largest television collection in the Archive is Ziv Television Library, a part of the United Artists gift. Ziv Television Programs, Inc., was the most successful producer and packager of dramatic programs for first-run syndicated use in the early days of television. Many of the Ziv series, such as Boston Blackie, Dr. Christian, and Highway Patrol, were the prototypes for now-standard genres in television programming. It was in these early series that stereotypical female roles (the understanding wife, the detective's secretary, the kindly doctor's nurse) were all refined for television. The Ziv Library, a total of 2,000 prints and negatives for thirty-eight television series from 1948 to 1962, is supplemented by scripts for these and twenty-nine additional series from the same time period. A departure from these stereotypes is afforded by the television programming available through the MTM Enterprises Collection. Selected films and videotapes from The Mary Tyler Moore Show, Rhoda, The Bob Newhart Show, and other MTM series, notable for their high production quality and the candor of their content, are held by the Center. In addition to these representative episodes, scripts from the series of MTM Enterprises are also available. Using materials from the Ziv Television Library and the MTM Collection, as well as a variety of smaller television collections, it is possible to trace the evolution of the image of women put forth by American television from its beginning to the present.

Publicity and exploitation are essential aspects of the entertainment business. As soon as the "star system" was formulated around 1912, each studio acquired a staff of hard-working publicity people whose express purpose was to perpetuate that system: making and sustaining images for the American public to devour. An examination of the publicity stills and the pressbooks which were created by the exploitation staff reveals how Hollywood studios saw their actresses, and how they intended the audience to see them. In the course of her career, an actress would have thousands of publicity photos taken and distributed to theaters and newspapers throughout the country. These photos document the studio's molding of an actress's public image--from "cheesecake" to elaborate costumes to painstakingly fabricated "home life" poses. The Center holds an expanding file of hundreds of thousands of these photographs, indexed by name of personality, which has been compiled from the collections of Daniel Blum, United Artists, and the Stein-Liebowitz-Schwart donation, as well as many other smaller collections.

Another duty of the studio's publicity and exploitation staff was to generate pressbooks designed for distribution to local theaters in advance of the arrival of a particular film. Each pressbook contains examples of posters which the theater owner could obtain to advertise the forthcoming films, as well as several pages of pre-written newspaper articles concerning the stars and filming of the picture, aimed at the local newspapers. The pressbook also provided the theater owner with ideas for elaborate publicity campaigns suited to the peculiarities of the region in which the film was to be shown. Since the main concern of any publicity department is "image," the pressbooks provide an unparalleled opportunity to study Hollywood's most forthright expression of its perception of women. The Center has thousands of pressbooks on file dating from the 'teens to the seventies, indexed by title of film.

The Center can provide the researcher with continuous-tone copies of photographs and photographic reproductions of material in the collections, but permission to reproduce or publish materials must be obtained from the copyright owner.

AFTERWORD

A dramatic change in the status of women in society has occurred over the last twenty years, a change that has affected the questions posed by historians. The view of Barbara Welter in the introduction to The Woman Question in American History (1973) criticized the state of traditional scholarship at that time. She noted that "Women in American history...are likely to be discussed abstractly as cosmic forces, or...as lonely over-achievers." Today the views of Gerda Lerner, a founder of the study of women's history, reflect the more advanced progress in the field. Lerner was appointed Robinson-Edwards Professor of History at the University of Wisconsin in 1981, the same year in which she took office as president of the Organization of American Historians, the first woman since Louise Phelps Kellogg to hold this position. In her recent pamphlet Teaching Women's History, Professor Lerner notes: "There is no women's history separate and unconnected from 'men's history'.... But history, as traditionally interpreted and recorded by historians, has been, in fact, the history of the activities of men ordered by male values." To change this historical pattern, historians must engage in a reconstruction of the past in order to produce analysis appropriate to the experiences of women. Women's history will grow as specific studies are completed, and in the future a synthesis with traditional history will occur; but for the present the task is discovery and interpretation of the missing element--women--as has been occurring for black, labor, Native

American, and Hispanic American history. Even though a tremendous amount of research remains to be done in the field of women's history, the words of Reuben Gold Thwaites on the occasion of the Society's building dedication in 1900 are an appropriate charge: "We are but on the threshold of possibilities...."

APPENDIX

Published Guides to Archival and Manuscript
Collections at the Society's Area Research Centers

EAU CLAIRE   <u>Guide to Archives and Manuscripts
                     in the Chippewa Valley Museum, Eau
                     Claire Public Library, University
                     of Wisconsin-Eau Claire Area Re-
                     search Center & Archives</u>. Madison,
                     The State Historical Society of Wis-
                     consin, 1977. Pp. 68. (Supersedes
                     1967 Checklist.)

GREEN BAY   <u>Guide to Archives and Manuscripts
                     in the University of Wisconsin-Green
                     Bay Area Research Center</u>/John A.
                     Fleckner, compiler. Madison, The
                     State Historical Society of Wiscon-
                     sin, 1978. Pp. 51. (Supersedes
                     1972 and 1976 Checklists.)

LA CROSSE   <u>Checklist of Archives and Manu-
                     scripts Holdings in the Wisconsin
                     State University-La Crosse Area
                     Research Center</u>. Madison, The State
                     Historical Society of Wisconsin,
                     1969. Pp. 29. [Out of print.]

MILWAUKEE   <u>Guide to Historical Resources in
                     Milwaukee Area Archives</u>/John A.
                     Fleckner and Stanley Mallach, edi-
                     tors. Milwaukee, Milwaukee Area
                     Archives Group, 1976. Pp. ix, 102.

	(Supersedes 1969 and 1973 Checklists.)
OSHKOSH	Checklist of Archives and Manuscripts Holdings in the Wisconsin State University-Oshkosh Area Research Center. Madison, The State Historical Society of Wisconsin, 1967. Pp. 30. [Out of print.]
PARKSIDE	Checklist of Archives and Manuscripts in the University of Wisconsin-Parkside Area Research Center. Madison, The State Historical Society of Wisconsin, 1977. Pp. 73. (Supersedes 1974 Checklist.)
PLATTEVILLE	Guide to the Archives & Manuscripts in the University of Wisconsin-Platteville Area Research Center/ Kathryn Otto, compiler. Madison, The State Historical Society of Wisconsin, 1978. Pp. 71. (Supersedes 1966 Selected Acquisitions.)
RIVER FALLS	Guide to the Archives and Manuscripts in the University of Wisconsin-River Falls Area Research Center. Madison, The State Historical Society of Wisconsin, 1975. Pp. 69. [Out of print.]
STOUT	Guide to Archives and Manuscripts in the University of Wisconsin-Stout Area Research Center/Gayle Martinson, compiler. Madison, The State Historical Society of Wisconsin, 1978. Pp. 25.
STEVENS POINT	Guide to Archives and Manuscripts in

the University of Wisconsin-Stevens
Point Area Research Center. Madison, The State Historical Society
of Wisconsin, 1978. Pp. 53. (Supersedes 1971 Checklist.)

ABOUT THE CONTRIBUTORS

This publication had its origins in a series of classroom presentations prepared at the request of Professor Diane L. Lindstrom for her graduate seminar in women's history at the University of Wisconsin-Madison in the spring of 1975.

James Danky, Newspapers and Periodicals Librarian; Chris Rongone, Archivist; Beverly Youtz, late Government Publications Reference Librarian; Christine Schelshorn, Photo Archivist, State Historical Society of Wisconsin; and Maxine Fleckner, Film Archivist, Wisconsin Center for Film and Theater Research, prepared this fourth edition.

The authors wish to thank members of the Editorial Division of the Society for their assistance in the production of all four editions of this pamphlet. We would also like to thank these Society staff members, past and present, for their help in preparing various sections of the publication: Joan Severa, James L. Hansen, Janis Clark, Josephine L. Harper, and Max Evans.

Ref
Z
7961
A1
W57
1982

APR 7 1983